Support for Coach J

"Coach Mo is an extremely passionate and humble coach. He poured confidence into me and taught me that culture is what makes a good team great. You must be willing to sacrifice for the greater good so that everyone can reach their common goal—which is winning a championship. The standard has to be set and met every single day. Coach Mo would always say, "How you do anything is how you do everything." He helped me to develop into a better player, and more importantly, a better man."
::Daniel Rahama - Former Player

"Coach Sumter is one of the best in the business when it comes to creating and maintaining a culture of success. He really knows what it takes to establish good team chemistry in a program."
::Coach Bill Broderick - Christopher Newport University Women's Basketball Head Coach

"True coaches should focus on effort rather than winning. If you give 100% effort and 100% energy 100% of the time, then the scoreboard will take care of itself."
::Dr. Earl Levingston - Coach, Author, and University of North Texas Professor

"I think that culture is the foundation of any program. Your success is based on how strong your culture is. Culture is accountability."
::Coach Jeff Battle - Providence College Associate Head Basketball Coach

"Coach Sumter has all the qualities to become a great coach. He has always been a competitor, a good listener, and very humble. He just keeps getting better.

The culture of a good team is to have talent that doesn't let their egos diminish any aspect of winning. Understanding when to use that talent or trust your teammates is so important!"
::Coach Chavez Mabry - Virginia State University Head Tennis Coach

"A team's culture should exemplify each player's values, attitudes, and goals about their sport, competition, and relationships with fellow players and coaches. A positive team culture gives players a reason to put forth their best effort. A strong team culture positively impacts the players and their performance. For players to trust each other on the court or field, they must feel like they are looking out for each other and have each other's back."
::Keith Goganious - Retired NFL Player

Do It 4 The CULTURE

Do It 4 The CULTURE
Achieving Maximum Mental Performance

By: Maurice "Mo" Sumter
Championship Coach

Copyright © 2023 Maurice Sumter.

All rights reserved. No part of this publication may be reproduced, distributed, or transmitted in any form or by any means, including photocopying, recording, or other electronic or mechanical methods, without the prior written permission of the publisher, except in the case of brief quotations embodied in critical reviews and certain other noncommercial uses permitted by copyright law. For permission requests, write to the publisher, addressed "Attention: Permissions Coordinator," to the email below.

45VISIONS@gmail.com

Contact: @M45Coach (Instagram & Twitter)

ISBN: 979-8-218-16926-8 (Paperback)

Any references to historical events, real people, or real places are used fictitiously. Names, characters, and places are products of the author's imagination.

Cover design by The Athlete's Nexus.

First printing edition 2023. POD by KDP Amazon.

DEDICATION

To my grandmother Evangelist Hattie Kindred & my mother Nancy Sanders

My grandmother was one of the most impactful women I have ever met. As a devout follower of God, she raised nine children, five nieces, two nephews, and a host of grandchildren. We had a unique way of living that shaped the core of my being. My grandmother had a powerful energy that I watched thousands of people gravitate toward. From helping the less fortunate to singing and dancing in the middle of the mall, to picking beans in the fields of Virginia, my grandmother knew about creating a culture of wealth. Not monetary but intellectual wealth. And, she shared it freely with those around her. Her impact on the community, her village, and anyone in range of her voice was very apparent at her funeral at the age of 94 where there was standing room only. This is still the most attended funeral I've witnessed as a child and as an adult.

My grandmother was the head and creator of our culture. She led our family with compassion, love, energy, and respect. She had expectations and a standard for how we were to conduct ourselves. She encouraged us, humbled us, cheered us on, challenged us, and watched us blossom. She coached us to be the best we could be by doing what she did to exemplify our culture.

One of the women spawned from the great Hattie Kindred was my mother, Nancy Sumter. My mother is special. I used to think it was just what mothers do for their children, especially when there is no patriarch. At 25, a thought hit me. I started thinking about how I process life and who I talk to the most, who I confide in, and who has been there for my biggest moments. It all dawned on me (through maturity or intentional observation) that my mother is amazing. She does it all, just like my grandmother. I often feel guilty that I can't love her more than I already do.

My mother's #1 rule was: "Good boys get everything, and bad boys get nothing." Her #2 rule was: "Somebody is always watching." I still turn to these rules when negative intentions creep into my thoughts. Knowing that someone was always watching made me very conscious of how I presented myself to the world. In fact, the title of this book is derived from this concept of thinking outside of yourself. Doing things as if your mom, your grandmother, your children, or whomever you consider a part of your village were watching. Do it on principle, as a way of life. Do it for the outcome you desire to achieve. My mother had me at 19, and now she has raised a college graduate, champion coach, and author. My mother is a light to this world, my grandmother was the sun, and I just want to be a ray of light that can enlighten someone to help them see their path to greatness established by their culture.

TABLE OF CONTENTS

FOREWORD……………………………………………..…1

PREFACE……………………………………...……………..5

PRE-SEASON………………………………………....…11

    I. SELFLESSNESS……………………………….....14
    II. DISCIPLINE……………………………………….18
    III. TIME MANAGEMENT……………………..….22
    IV. RESPONSIBILITY & ACCOUNTABILITY…...25
    V. SMALL CIRCLE……………………………….…29
    VI. CHAMPIONSHIP EFFORT………….…..……..33
    VII. EMBRACING THE PROCESS……...…..…....38

SEASON………………………………………………....43

    I. SELFLESSNESS……………………………….....46
    II. DISCIPLINE……………………………………….51
    III. TIME MANAGEMENT……………………..….54
    IV. RESPONSIBILITY & ACCOUNTABILITY…...58
    V. SMALL CIRCLE……………………………….…62
    VI. CHAMPIONSHIP EFFORT………….…..……..68
    VII. EMBRACING THE PROCESS……...…..…....73

POST-SEASON……………………………………………77

OVERTIME………………………………………………83

ABOUT THE AUTHOR……….…..……………………...91

FOREWORD

By: Tamara Joy Hunter, M. ED.
-Golden Apple Peer Collaborative Coach.
Lee County School District

Here we are! You have crossed into another arena of success and my heart swells with pride and joy. I still remember the days when we were young, growing up together under the loving embrace of our village. Though we were cousins by blood, we called each other siblings because our bond went far beyond mere family ties. We were raised with a village mentality, where caring for one another, offering guidance during difficult times, and knowing that we were deeply loved were the foundations of our upbringing.

In our family, we were nurtured by the collective effort of our loved ones—who poured their morals, values, and faith into our hearts. Our grandparents, our mothers—Lina and Nancy—and the plethora of aunts and uncles who surrounded us had high expectations for us, teaching us the invaluable lesson of "each one, teach one" with very little financial means. We grew up knowing that we were part of something greater and that our actions and choices had the power to shape not only our own lives but also the lives of those who would follow in our footsteps.

You, my Reecie, have always been an inspiration to me and the next generation of children in our family. With your unwavering determination and boundless dreams, you exemplify a growth mindset that knows no limits. From the early days when you showcased your talents as a sweet little honor student rapping and dancing in the midst of close friends, to the moments when you took on the role of team captain, motivating and uplifting football and basketball teams, you have always embraced the pursuit of greatness.

Your achievements speak for themselves, from being recognized as one of the "Greatest Top 5 Players" in Longwood University history and a professional basketball player overseas, to coaching at various Division 1 colleges. But what truly sets you apart is your ability to build a positive culture of success wherever you go. You understand that true achievement lies not only in personal goals but also in uplifting others and creating a supportive foundation for those around you. Your commitment to pouring into the children of our future demonstrates the depths of your character and the love that
radiates from within you.

I am proud of the man you have become. Your seasons have been filled with triumphs and challenges, and through it all, you have remained steadfast in "I am Greater Than…" in your pursuit of excellence. As I reflect on our shared memories and the lessons we learned in Ocean View, Huntersville, and Norview, I am certain that your book will inspire and ignite the hearts of those who read it to grow!

May your words serve as a beacon of hope, reminding us all of the transformative power of culture and the importance of cherishing our collective heritage. Your experiences, your wisdom, and your
unwavering love for our family and community will undoubtedly leave an undeniable mark on the generations to

come. Your shoulders will become the foundation on which they stand as they conquer
their own goals and dreams.

Know that as your oldest sibling and constant supporter, I will love you forever. Your journey is one of resilience, determination, and unwavering belief. As you continue to soar, may your light shine bright, and may your book become a guiding star for all those who seek to understand the beauty and significance of doing it for the culture.

K.I.M. (Keep it Moving)

PREFACE

Everybody wants to be a winner. The goal of this book is to help leaders build a championship culture through conversations, activity prompts, and mind exercises. If these strategies are followed and implemented, it will raise the mental capacity, mental fortitude, and preparation of any group or individual for the intense journey to success. As I prepared to write, I realized that this mentality can be applied in sports, business, or any form of leadership. Being a champion at every level of sports (high school, college, and professional) as both a player and a coach, has given me insight into what it takes to build a championship culture for long-term success. I felt it was necessary to share what I learned with others as a roadmap to the ultimate goal: SUCCESS.

The title of this book is: *Do It 4 the Culture*. What is Culture? Culture is the foundation of any success or failure. It is the written and unwritten rules that we abide by that take us down the path to our goal. It's the way we do things that send messages and sets the bar for expected behavior. Culture includes our habits and directs our energy and emotion toward our goals. Culture is the embodiment of the group where everyone takes ownership of the outcome before the journey begins. It is what cultivates talent or hinders it. We are all simply the product of the culture that we establish and accept.

In any situation where there are goals, expectations, winners, and losers, there is culture. In this book, I used the basketball season as the context to display the thought processes and behaviors conducive to winning and success. I have established seven pillars that symbolize important elements of a winning and results-driven culture. Each pillar has its own conversation and talking points for both leaders and followers. This is where you establish the expectations for your team or group. The seven pillars are:

1. **Selflessness**
2. **Discipline**
3. **Time Management**
4. **Responsibility and Accountability**
5. **Small Circle**
6. **Championship Effort**
7. **Embracing the Process**

As you learn how to implement each pillar into your culture, this book will outline how these factors contribute to your success. There will be a *Breakdown* section in each chapter, which will explain what each pillar's intentions are and what you should aim to get from each concept. The *Story* is a real situation that I've encountered or witnessed that relates to the pillar. The *Summary* is a recap of the pillar and its relationship to success.

There are also *3 R's* that are explained at the end of each chapter. The 3 R's are included to *Remind* readers of the importance of the pillar, describe the *Routine* or call to action that the pillar establishes, and the *Reward* that your program or organization will gain from executing this pillar properly.

In most sports, the season is broken down into 3 major parts: The Preseason, Season, and Postseason. Throughout these time periods, success requires a different mental approach to help you maximize time and effort.

Pre-Season

The goal of the Preseason is to set the tone of your foundation, build mental and physical endurance, push you past your limits, and prepare you for the wear and tear of the grueling season that lies ahead. It is where you break down the goals you have set into small individual parts and sharpen them. This is where you are learning your strengths and weaknesses and identifying roles. Similarly in business, this is the time you sit at the table and assign different tasks and responsibilities to people according to their strengths, titles, and skills. This is when you establish what you want to get out of those jobs in preparation for the presentation. Everyone learns their roles and how to maximize their strengths to help the team get the best results.

Throughout the pillars of the Preseason, you will gain direction in your conversations as you build what's needed for this time of year. The goal is to build endurance both physically and mentally. This is where the foundation begins.

Season

The Season requires a different mindset. You are now bringing all the breakdowns, the skills, and the grit of the Preseason together and forming your style of play. Mentally, you transition to a more team-oriented focus rather than a focus on individual contributions to the goal. At this point in the process, you will have games or opportunities to present what you know. The season is when you are tested.

Accountability is a major factor in growth. Your goal is to create a space where players feel comfortable being wrong and have the will to correct it. Conversations about players' roles and how they can help the team will bring clarity. Players must embrace that role and work to expand it with consistency. Consistency breeds trust.

It is important to consider what the players are saying to themselves as the ups and downs of the season take their toll. A season is a marathon. Motivation, confidence, and anxiety management must be solidified in their minds. During the season, there must be constant reminders and reiterations of what was built in the Preseason through repetition and correction. Again, the Preseason is where this foundation is established.

There are a lot of distractions during the Season. The people around the players are some of the most influential voices they hear. These people do not see the daily work behind the scenes. Yet, they will whisper to the player what *they* believe the results should be. It is the responsibility of both the player and the coach to have a clear understanding of what success looks like for THEM. The refs, fans, family, friends, former coaches, and significant others are all distractions that will pull on their mind space. It's a battle to remain focused on the championship mentality along with everything else going on in their lives. This section of the book is designed to guide you through the conversations and mindset shifts needed for high-level focus, whether that's a championship game or a business acquisition.

Post-Season

The Post-Season is when self-evaluations happen. It is designed to guide conversations of accountability while assessing the season from the player's perspective. What you see and what they see are often totally different. This Post-Season process will expose critical items, give players the opportunity to verbalize their experiences and give coaches insight into how to adjust their success strategy. You will find that players may act as if it's someone or something outside of themselves impacting their outcomes, when in fact it was themselves. And, they know it.

Instead of telling them how their season was, help them revisit their positives and missteps. They will get to gauge what works and what doesn't. They will get to express what their bars of success and failure are. You get to step into their world and see their perspective. As a leader or coach, you will get the opportunity to hear what they think about you as well as how you are executing your vision. It's both healthy and informative. Then, you provide notes on the next steps for them to improve and become the performer you believe can help the team at some point in the future.

Culture is the formula for success and failure. It is the foundation of all teams, groups, or companies. There are no exact sciences or magic formulas. But, from my experiences and observations, there are consistencies that hold true to team success. The people involved must feel ownership. They must feel like they affect the outcome. These pillars both empower and clarify.

PRE-SEASON

Pre-Season

1. Selflessness
2. Discipline
3. Time Management
4. Responsibility and Accountability
5. Small Circle
6. Championship Effort
7. Embracing the Process

This is the time of year that you are learning about your players and their limits. You are observing what makes them go and adapting your style to connect with them. This is also the time that you are instilling the critical pillars of your culture that will lead to success. For some players, the structure of a program will be new. For others, you will be reinforcing your principles and philosophies. During the Pre-Season, you will see leaders emerge and become the locker room voices that will be needed throughout the Season. The Pre-Season is when you build, instill, and cultivate your culture.

I. SELFLESSNESS

Breakdown

Selflessness is when you're concerned with others' needs and wishes as much, if not more, than your own. In order to concern yourself with others' needs, you have to know what their needs are. Which leads us to perspectives and points of view. Knowing why someone reacted the way they reacted is a huge part of selflessness if given the proper context. How many times have you taken something out of context or taken something personal yet felt differently after having the conversations of understanding? How the people around you think connects the minds and intentions of individuals to form a team or cohesive group. So, knowing how the people around you think can be a binding agent to success by allowing you to anticipate and be sensitive to their needs in the moment. There must be space to think and grow together when you share a common goal. Over time, everyone experiences some type of growth. The goal is to grow in the same direction. It's a constant battle of pride and conquering space in the mind. Selflessness comes more easily when we have mutual interests, goals, and intentions to be successful.

Culture Notes

1. Selflessness is the ability to see things from different vantage points at different times.

    - Why did that person make that decision?
    - What have they seen or gone through to make them feel, think, or act that way?

2. There is a difference between "rivalry" and "healthy competition."

    - Rivalry is cancerous; teammates are hoping other teammates fail.
    - The goal is to compete and not to "beat" the other teammate.
    - Never lose focus on the goal in the quest to win the matchup.

3. Trust the process! Character → Process → Results

    - The "private voice" (what you say to yourself in your head) can be an asset or a liability.
    - We must continually think positively to be ready mentally for the next play.
    - Negative thinking is a win for the opponent.
4. How you think is just as important as what you think.

    - You need to know how people under and around you process things. Pay attention to body language, public image, and social media.
    - Your awareness can help you respond appropriately to certain actions and behaviors.
    - Control the controllables...YOU!

5. You must win mind space!

- Everything flows from what and how the mind thinks.
- Allow space for new thoughts even if they are different than your own.
- Protect the space for those who have your best interest, even if you cannot see it.

Story

As I watched the "Malice in the Palace" Documentary, Jermain O'Neal (former NBA player) said something interesting: "If I knew what Ron Artest was going through, I would have handled him totally differently." That took me back to one of my players. He was one of the hardest-working and most disciplined players I've ever coached. We would workout 1-on-1, sit and talk, and exchange texts for years. I gave him pointers on life, school and basketball. We talked one day in an individual meeting, and I asked him about his family. He told me he had two brothers and a sister. His dad had died two years prior to that conversation and his mother had moved back to Africa. Unfortunately, they did not communicate consistently. It hurt me to know that I was coaching him for a full year and had no idea he had no access to his parents. It changed my approach to getting to know both players and recruits.

Summary

Perspective is everything and nothing at the same time. So, when it comes to being selfless, you have to account for both the perspective of the other person and your own. The balance of the two is the ultimate level of selflessness.

Why we react the way we react or make the decisions we make are a result of how we perceive what someone else was thinking and/or their intentions. When you are establishing a common goal, it is important to know how others around you think. You must be aware of their intentions so that your actions will align. Everything that you watch, observe, read, see, and scroll through is in a constant battle for your mind space. When leaders build a winning culture, it is important to allow space for different thoughts and perspectives to understand the team's motivations to succeed. Even as a coach, we must be open to learn as we lead people to an unknown place. We must value their perspectives as much as our own.

"3 R's of Selflessness"

Reminder: Selflessness is important because it helps players be accountable to each other. The hope is that you build a culture of players who want success for those around them as much as for themselves.

Routine: In order to celebrate others' success, you have to know what success looks like for THEM. Have players write their goals down and exchange them with a teammate. The exchange is to get them to hold each other accountable to the goals THEY set for THEMSELVES.

Reward: The reward of instilling this pillar into your culture is seeing your players get excited when their teammate progresses on something they couldn't do initially or have been working hard on. They will be proud to see their brother or sister overcome an obstacle. They feel a sense of accomplishment just being on the ride with them.

II. DISCIPLINE

Breakdown

Discipline is a consistent act or mindset even when the circumstances vary. It's doing and not doing. It's going hard for a goal or target and being patient enough to fall back when needed. Whining, complaining, and making excuses are not parts of discipline. There is not a lot of wiggle room or any exemptions. Doing things to the best of your ability every time, whether that's making your bed or touching the line on a sprint. This discipline is shown in the most adverse times for a team or group. A disciplined team will be consistent with their efforts and body language if they're up 20 points or down 20 points. People often call the minutes after the game has been decided "garbage time," but it's an important display of the true discipline of your team. Setting goals is a cheat sheet for discipline. It holds you to tangible accountability and helps track progress (or lack thereof).

Culture Notes

1. Discipline is the practice of training people to consistently obey rules or a code of behavior.

    - It is important to establish expectations as guidelines to help the team reach its goal.
    - You can use consequences to correct or command behavior.
    - Be patient and remember that the end goal is the result of smaller, consistent steps.

2. Always believe that things will work out as long as we do the things we should in the right way.

    - Do not whine, complain, or make excuses.
    - Do things to the best of your ability every time.
    - Know that things happen because you work toward them consistently not because you want them.

3. You must set goals and actively pursue them. This helps you avoid distractions.

    - Written goals have a higher chance of being kept and achieved.
    - Make sure that your goals are meaningful and that they are specific and measurable.
    - Create a plan, including daily actions, that must be taken to achieve your goals.
    - Track progress through scheduled monthly, weekly, and daily check-ins.

4. Organization is an indicator of discipline!

    - Discipline is a habit. You should see it in your life on and off the court.
    - Improve discipline incrementally, by improving one small thing each day. For example, once you are done using something, put it back where it belongs as soon as you finish using it.
    - Once your physical space is organized, your mind will be more relaxed and able to focus.

Story

In 2018 and 2019, we emphasized doing things the right way every time—not depending on how tired you are, the time of day, or the weather. Doing it right for the sole reason of it being RIGHT. Discipline is a habit, a mental state that creates consistency in everything you do. This gives you the ability to execute and be consistent. One of our rules as a team was, we never split the pole. The entire team bought into this principle. This was not because we were superstitious, but because we did not want to take any chances. One time, ten of our players went on one side of the double doors and one didn't. Do you want to guess what we did? Our whole team went back around so that they all could walk through the same side as one. It may have appeared to be a game or superstition to the untrained eye, but it was much deeper. It was a discipline, a consistency of us doing things together as one and it translated onto the court. One of my coaches always said, "If we are all doing it wrong, then we are all right."

Summary

You can do anything in the world if you can be consistent and disciplined. The "Discipline" pillar aims to clarify the mindset of discipline. It's a full-time and all-inclusive mind state. The more facets of your life in which you can exercise these two giants, the closer you will be to your goal. Being organized and having a clear goal will clear the path to wherever it is you aspire to be. If you and your team or group can make the path visual and clear for all, success is often right around the corner. Anything you work at consistently with discipline, you will become good at.

Now, that holds for both good and bad habits. Whatever you practice you will improve. Your habits are what define you.

"3 R's of Discipline"

Reminder. This pillar may be the most important. Discipline creates consistency, and consistency creates success. This is important because it encourages you to do things the right way every time. No matter your mood, feeling, or any other distraction. Just because that's the way it's supposed to be done. It sets the bar and then you adjust/improve.

Routine. You must be deliberate and consistent with the little things on and off the court. They are the big things. It's important to build the core thinking of doing things right no matter what it is. It translates to the court when you build the person. Then, it becomes habitual to the point where players won't feel right if they don't do the thing in the right way. One example is to set a pre-practice routine.

Reward. The reward is the translation into success of everything you do. The reward is the achievement of the goal. Doing things right and to the best of your ability becomes habitual. It's a mindset that you are trying to build and makes the outcome more consistent and predictable.

III. TIME MANAGEMENT

Breakdown

The most valuable asset of all is time. Time is even more valuable than money. You can get money, give it away, and make it again. However, time doesn't have that same flexibility. Time is linear; it goes in one direction, and it is uninterrupted and continuous. You should value time more than any other facet of life. If you don't value others' time, they will devalue "YOU." When you don't value others' time, it shows carelessness and gives the appearance of selfishness. Carelessness and selfishness are two of the lowest qualities a teammate can have. On the other hand, preparation shows the ultimate value of time. It is the ultimate showing of valuing others.

Culture Notes

1. The most valuable asset of all is time.

    - You must value your time AND the time of others.
    - Every minute and every second counts, because they should be used to get closer to the long-term outcome.

2. It is inconsiderate to make people wait for you.

    - It shows carelessness, a lack of empathy, and selfishness.

3. It takes time to put yourself in a position to succeed.

    - Proper preparation prevents poor performance.

4. Discipline is a reflection of how you spend your time.

    - You must do things the right way when no one is looking.
    - You must be able to look beyond the current moment and see how your actions will affect the next moment.
    - When managing your time, you must consider all possible outcomes while sticking to the plan.
    - Over time, being on time will build trust, reliability, and accountability.

<u>Story</u>

I am a true believer in "how you do anything, is how you do everything." Being on time for anything—such as practice, meetings and games—says a lot to a coach or boss. While coaching at a ranked school and coming off a record-setting season, our staff felt we needed to get better. We brought in a player who was more than talented enough to be a starter if not a leading scorer. A part of his pattern of behavior was to be late, right on time, or barely making his classes and meetings. Once the season came, you guessed it, he was late for practices and always had a reason to not be there. It wasn't until he changed his preparation and time management that he was able to reach his full potential as a player, a father, and a person—and we were able to reach our goals for him as a team.

Summary

We all value money, for some it's first or second on their list of important things. But I ask, if YOU had to choose between time and money, which one is more valuable to you? How you spend your time says so much about you as a person. How you value others' time speaks to how much you value them. Preparation either gives you a head start, or the lack thereof puts you behind before you even begin. Preparation can also give you confidence and the space to have room for error. Each day is a new day, but it is still connected to yesterday and tomorrow. We do not know how much time we have left, but what we do know is that each second, minute, day, week, month, year, and decade that goes by gets us closer to the end.

"3 R's of Time Management"

Reminder. Everything, including sports, has a set time or season. So, time—down to the second—matters. Time must be a priority because it makes a difference in all outcomes.

Routine. There should be a hard stance on time. Where we are and when we are there can be practiced or rehearsed every day. Set the time; set the consequence.

Reward. The reward from this step is trust and reliability. They must all know where to be and when they should be there. You can think and act more freely which makes you respond faster and be more effective.

IV. RESPONSIBILITY & ACCOUNTABILITY

Breakdown

What does Responsibility and Accountability mean to you? You are responsible for your actions, interactions, and reactions. Whatever you do as a person, as a player, or as a teammate is your responsibility. There is nobody else to blame; you are in control of you, and nobody can force you to do anything. Being responsible means you take ownership of your actions and reactions. If others can make you do something and you find yourself blaming them for what you did, then being responsible is a weakness for you. On the other hand, accountability is your willingness to hold yourself responsible for your actions and reactions regardless of the circumstances. When you are accountable, you will grow from what you learn and go through. This sets a standard for yourself and those around you as you learn who you are based on how you respond to certain situations.

Culture Notes

1. Winners take responsibility for their actions and hold themselves accountable to their teammates.

    - Responsibility- The state or fact of having a duty to deal with something or of having control over someone. The opportunity or ability to act independently and make decisions without authorization.
    - Accountability- The fact or condition of being accountable; required or expected to

justify actions or decisions.

2. Identify what you are known for.

- Be known for what you stand for. You should be able to clearly articulate what is important to you.
- Do not focus on what you are "against." This introduces a negative state of thinking. Establishing what you support is the catalyst to commitment.

3. Know who you are so you can play to your strengths.

- You are more coachable when you play to your strengths.
- You are more forgiving of your mistakes when you play to your strengths.
- You are more self-aware of your weaknesses.

Story

Have you ever said, "he/she almost made me _____" or "he/she made me mad?" I have heard my players say that from time to time. These statements usually preclude the times that you are almost about to submit your control. I have worked with players of all ages and usually the reason they say something went wrong was because of a reaction to somebody else or some outside force. In these scenarios, what is actually happening is these players are handing their control of the outcome and control of their lives to someone else. While they were trying to control the situation, they were actually doing the opposite by giving control to someone else and allowing them to control the outcome.

Summary

Being responsible and accountable is you taking and commanding control of your life and future. When you invest in controlling your inner self, you will possess more control of the world and the outcomes around you. If you look at any situation you have gone through, you can probably point to a moment or a decision where your actions affected the outcome of the situation. Look within.

"3 R's of Responsibility & Accountability"

Reminder. This pillar is important, because being responsible and accountable strips you of your ego and allows you the ability to be wrong and grow from mistakes. You become coachable.

Routine. Explaining the "what" and the "why" creates clear communication about the mission. Once the goal is established in some verbal or written contract, there are no excuses for any deviation from the plan. Either you got it done or you didn't. Actually, there are three options: 1) You did it. There is nothing to say when your actions speak. 2). You can do it but did not. This is usually a sign of a lack of discipline. 3) You cannot do it. In this case, the leader must find someone else who can.

Reward. The reward you will get from creating a culture of responsibility and accountability will be a team that holds themselves and each other accountable to the pillars of the culture that will make you all successful. This trust is essential in a winning culture.

V. SMALL CIRCLE

Breakdown

Keeping a small circle is not just meant to keep people out but to keep what you have in. The goal is to create a safe and trusting environment, where you can feel safe being wrong, making a mistake, or just being your authentic self. You have to be aware of the energy around you or you risk compromising the stability of your ship. Most athletes learn that egos are both a gift and a curse when competing. People will feed your ego and cause you to lose sight of the goal. Sometimes, you have to maintain your confidence with thousands of fans telling you how much of a failure you are. But, ego is also what makes you so good.

The problems arise when you have trouble turning your ego off. It is especially hard when the people around you are feeding that type of toxicity. However, in defense of all athletes, we are not taught how to handle that aspect of our lives. We sometimes behave differently with our families than we do with our peers. We try to prove things to our peers. But, with family, we know there is authentic love around us, and this safe and comfortable place allows us to grow and be more willing to listen. In your small circle, you can just be yourself and be vulnerable.

Culture Notes

1. The objective of having a small circle is to create an environment where you and your team feels emotionally safe enough to take responsibility for error.

- When the circle is not tight, players will lie to each other and hide their authentic selves.
- This can create distrust that translates into games.

2. While you want to keep a small circle, the things outside your "world" can help you grow and expand your mindset.

- Family can be a source of growth in certain situations.
- External people and factors can help you better understand your situation and better understand others.

3. It's just as important to identify where we're **not** as much as it is to identify where we are.

- Clearly identify why you do not spend time with certain people, in certain places, and in certain situations.
- Do not give negative people your energy; they will disrupt your winning culture.
- Too many people around is excess and excess is wasteful.

Story

Having a small circle requires you to take into account who you are listening to. It may appear that adults and people in position of power have the best interest of the athletes. Unfortunately, that is not always the case. One team I was a part of had a culture of players congregating in a particular location on campus. In some of the conversations, some of the players would share private, intimate information with people outside the team. This breach of trust caused tension between players and coaches alike.

People outside of the team circle can be detrimental to trust-building and the camaraderie of the team. You must feel emotionally safe to be vulnerable and grow, and that usually happens when you keep a small circle. If people who are allowed to infiltrate your small circle are not echoing the coaches' or the cultures' sentiments, it will be impossible for the players within the group to be on the same page. At some point, there will be a disconnect.

Summary

We all want to be loved, liked, and accepted. What we don't like to feel is rejection. For most, that seems to be an internal battle. Now, put 20 egos in one room jockeying to be loved, liked, and accepted. There will be endless bravado. The goal of having a small circle is to create an environment of trust amongst egos. Wanting success for the person beside you as you pursue success for yourself. It is imperative to take one common goal and to put that above personal drama, insecurity, and selfishness. It may be hard to grasp, but what comes of this culture pillar is complete investment in protecting the team's success.

"3 R's of Small Circle"

Reminder. This pillar is important because it minimizes distractions. Keep the space safe to embrace the culture. The less outside voices that your players listen to, the more likely they are to listen to you. In the battle for mind space, the more that you can immerse them into the culture, the closer you get to success.

Routine. Continue to stress that who they are spending their time with and listening to affects the way they approach the mission. Have conversations with your team individually to understand who is important to them and why. These relationships usually reveal why they react to things the way they do.

Reward. Your goal is to get your team to make the team goals and success a priority over any personal ambitions or outside distractions.

VI. CHAMPIONSHIP EFFORT

Breakdown

There is a numerical breakdown that can be used to describe most teams or groups: 10-80-10. The first 10% are the ones who will do the work most of the time or to the best of their ability. The next 80% will do what is necessary most times, depending on how they feel or the details of the situation. The last 10% will usually fail to do the right thing or what is necessary for many reasons. Therein, lies commitment issues. The goal is to pull the 80% into the first 10% and to pull the bottom 10% into the middle 80%. Always grow and make progress when you are cultivating championship effort.

The teams that slide this scale, especially in the direction of the first 10%, tend to have more success. Oftentimes, players wonder why their play is inconsistent which usually leads to their playing time being inconsistent. The reason is that our minds are habitual. So, essentially, when our work ethic is inconsistent, our results are inconsistent. You have to put yourself in a position to be "found." This means that your work ethic and preparation will determine who, what, when, where, and how success will be a part of your life. Consistent, maximum effort is in the DNA of a championship team.

Culture Notes

1. Learn the 10-80-10 rule to better understand how to help your players.

- **Top 10%:** These players are coachable and consistent, and they come ready to work every day.
- **Middle 80%:** These players are inconsistent and tend to exhibit a roller coaster of emotions. Day in and day out, it "depends" if and how they show up.
- **Bottom 10%:** These players usually carry a negative disposition and feel the world revolves around them. They may talk the most and try to negatively influence others.

2. When you are pursuing a championship effort through culture, there are two sides of pain.

    - You may suffer and feel discomfort. Some players may quit at the first sign of adversity. Some of this is generational, as many modern players create a habit of not finishing things.
    - You can also experience success and glory. Greatness is on the other side of pain.

3. You must put yourself in a place to be found. Championships find you when you put yourself in the right position.

    - You must earn your keep through hard work and consistent grind.
    - As a leader, you must encourage your players to stay focused on the prize.

4. You must create a culture of positivity and growth.

- Speak life. Words are like seeds; you give life to situations when you speak them.
- It is impossible to speak negatively and have a positive life. Your words become your reality.
- You reap what you sow. Your actions will align with your reward.

Story

Working with college athletes can be hard and humbling. They have egos; which is both the thing that makes them great and the thing that can hold them back the most. During a championship season run, we had players from both winning and losing programs at the Division I and Division II levels. The difference in the season was that the Top 10% pulled from the 80%, the 80% pulled from the bottom 10%, and they all did this by holding each other accountable for maximum effort every day. This culture brought more consistency, less excuses, and less blame. They wanted each other to be successful and celebrated each other's success. When it got painful, they had someone beside them to push and pull them through the pain. As a team, we put ourselves in a position to defeat a team by 30 points that had a future NBA player on its roster. The championship effort created a championship culture.

Summary

Championship effort is something that opens the door

for a championship to be earned. If this effort is not consistent, then championship-level success is hard to reach. The 10-80-10 rule, the sides of pain and putting yourself in position are always connected, because the rule separates the group. Pain is either a motivator or a hindrance; it can stop you or put you over the top. Once you understand which side you're on, that will determine what position you put yourself in. Will you be in a place or a space to take advantage of an opportunity? Or will you find an excuse or blame others for your outcome? You can only control the effort, but the effort opens the door to success.

"3 R's of Championship Effort"

Reminder. The championship effort pillar is important because it is the foundation of how you approach the goal. It's what gets the wheels going; it's putting the destination in your navigation. You must push past your limits to prepare for the most extreme conditions the road to success has to offer.

Routine. A routine is required to build the foundation of effort and repetition to do things at a high level over a long period of time—both physically and mentally. Mental endurance must be built every single day.

Reward. Your goal is to witness those high-level habits of consistency become instinctual. When you instill a culture of championship effort into your program, you allow success to find you.

VII. EMBRACING THE PROCESS

Breakdown

Every day is about getting better. The small steps equal big results. So, it is important when building the right foundation that you only add things that help promote growth. Staying focused on your "why" will help you avoid the distractions that derail success. But, know that you are building each and every day. Sometimes, it boils down to the simple competition of "You vs. You." You should never turn down an opportunity to learn and to get better. People do not realize that failure and obstacles are a part of the process, and they fuel growth. You get what you consistently earn.

Culture Notes

1. The process is reaffirmed on every play and every day.

    - Being committed to the process of getting better requires focus and concentration.
    - The ultimate goal of the process is to accomplish the team objective and not to feed individual egos (selfishness).

2. There are knowns (finite things) and unknowns (infinite things) that are a part of the process.

    - The finite things are the rules of the game, the players, and the team objectives. These things are expected and can be prepared for.
    - The infinite things are the injuries,

officiating, and outside influences. These unknowns are unpredictable, but they still must be prepared for.
- Control what you can control.

3. You must be obsessed with getting better while staying focused on your goals.

- Talent is naturally given, but skill is developed through hard work.
- The culture should encourage learning from others rather than just "beating" others.
- The best way to get to the next spot is to be great in the one you're in.

4. There are no excuses along the process to success.

- When you make excuses, you deny yourself of a learning opportunity.
- Fear ignites your courage and gives your obstacles credit.
- Success gives you peace of mind through self-satisfaction and self-actualization.

5. There are many elements of the process that must be embraced.

- After pushing the mind and body to its limits, recovery must include food, rest, and rehabilitation.
- You must be patient with the process and know that it is a marathon, not a sprint.

Story

I've been around coaches that care about different things that some may consider to be "small" or "minor." Things such as players wearing hats in the building, players styling their hair in certain ways, players tucking their practice jerseys in, and so on. What it all boils down to are the" little" disciplines that make or break a team or group. It's like a small hole in a canoe. It may take a while, but the water will at some point sink the boat. I have found that your weakness may not be noticeable to others throughout a successful regular season. But, it will always be the thing that is exploited in the postseason. Throughout one season I coached, our team struggled to exploit teams when they switched to a zone defense. When our team played in a game to go to the Sweet 16, our opponent played a zone defense the last four minutes of the game, hit a huge 3-pointer late in the game, and our historic season was ended.

Summary

Everybody wants to win the prize. Oftentimes, we see the celebration and image of that moment. The only problem is, everyone wants to skip the process and get straight to the confetti. The early morning workouts and the late-night bus rides are what makes the ring so special and memorable. Every "little" thing, such as showing up everyday, is all a piece of the process. If you take away enough bricks from the house, it will collapse. Those days, those processes, those "little" disciplines are bricks that build the foundation that make the house or culture. That culture will encompass and translate to the court, field, or place of business. Everything matters to everything else.

Think about it, how do you separate each team? By its processes. Every team is talented and has a coach with experience, shoots on the same level of hoop, with the same balls and refs. So, what separates them?? If you ask any coach, you will find out that the most talented teams win a lot less than you may think. It is usually the team that pushes each other, shows up every day, and holds each other accountable. They expect everyone to "earn their keep." Even the most talented players on the most talented teams will say how important "coming together" was to their success. The games are the test and the by-product of your process.

"3 R's of Embracing the Process"

Reminder. The "Embracing the Process" pillar is important because once you embrace the process, you will begin to understand your role and why it is important to the entire mission. You will know that the small steps you take toward success represent growth and progress.

Routine. The routine that you must follow for this pillar involves you constantly tracking progress and setting mini-goals along the way. This is where transparency is so important to everyone understanding their role in the process and holding one another accountable.

Reward. Your goal is to get your team to push each other through competition and to understand how that helps the team. You want to make sure the competition is channeled in the right direction. Your reward is to have your team embrace healthy competition on the road to success.

SEASON

Season

1. Selflessness
2. Discipline
3. Time Management
4. Responsibility and Accountability
5. Small Circle
6. Championship Effort
7. Embracing the Process

Once you have established a solid foundation for the culture within your program or your organization, you must be intentional about reinforcing the seven pillars. The most important difference between the Pre-Season and the Season is the degree of control and intensity in which you hold your players accountable to the expectations established within your culture. When it is time for the Season, the cream will rise. That is an old-fashioned way of saying the players who have earned your trust and that of their teammates typically play more and find more success.

In the Pre-Season, you must be firm about their adherence to team rules, behaviors, and philosophies. This is your introduction and teaching stage. During the Season, you want to remain firm but give your players space to adopt your principles and make them their own. This is the reinforcement stage. However, you must remain consistent in your rewards, discipline, and consequences. When the end-of-season championship run heats up, they will benefit from this space you are giving them to execute what they have learned. By this time of the year, your culture should be embedded and instinctual.

I. SELFLESSNESS

Breakdown

At this point in the year, it is important to continue building on the trust that has been established in the Pre-Season. Seeing things from others' perspectives is important when trying to accomplish a common goal. When you know their "why," you can communicate in their language. Knowing their "why" may make you want to help them get their "why" more than you want yours. In sports, there is always healthy competition within a team. But, the most important competition should be with your yesterday self. You can only control yourself and the daily mentality you approach the day with. To be selfless is to be open to new thoughts from people that have your mutual interest, such as teammates and family members. You cannot outperform someone beyond the success of the team. In many ways, positivity and positive self-talk can help the inner voice be more positive, and this will translate into how you communicate with others.

Culture Notes

1. Selflessness is the ability to see things from different vantage points at different times.

    - Why do certain players have certain tendencies?
    - What have they seen or gone through to make them feel, think, or act that way?

2. There is a difference between "rivalry" and "healthy competition."

    - Do your players root for one another with the same intensity that they compete against one another?
    - Do your players admit when they are wrong?
    - Do your players pick up the slack when playing with weaker players?

3. How you think is just as important as what you think.

    - You must read body language to learn situations that make your players uncomfortable. They may never admit their discomfort for fear of being viewed as "less than."
    - Watch how they respond in leadership situations to learn who your natural team leaders are. Their voices are important voices in the locker room and on the court.
    - Control what you can control…YOU!

4. You must win mind space!

    - As a leader, the way that you create more mind space for yourself is by listening to your players – what they say, what they don't say, and what they do.
    - As a leader, the way that you help your players create more mind space is by

encouraging them to share why they did certain things. Understanding another person's thoughts is a key component of selflessness.
- Even if people think differently, they must share a common goal.

5. Establishing a "mistake ritual" is an easy way to build the selflessness pillar.

- Every player must be invested in getting one another through mistakes.
- Help teammates recover and rebound from mistakes by encouraging positive talk between your players. When someone makes a mistake, there should be multiple teammates saying, "You're good!" "Get it back." "You got this!"

Story

As the leader of most teams I have been a part of as a player and coach, I've always felt it was my job to hold myself and my teammates accountable. To do so, I had to learn what motivates each of them and how to deliver on that motivation. I would be aggressive with some teammates, and some I had to take a gentler approach. I had to give other teammates outward encouragement when they did something good – almost in a child-like way. There have been some teammates that I have had to remind about their "why."

Over time, I paid attention to how they responded to being held accountable or accepting constructive criticism. This showed me how to get the best out of them. As a coach, it is also important to be selfless with my players and consider what makes them tick. But, in order to invest time into learning another person and understanding their tendencies and preferences, I had to be aware of the inner conversations that I have with myself. The "self" in selflessness has been a significant factor in making me a better and more coachable coach in all settings.

Summary

It is often the simple gestures that make the most difference, such as encouraging a teammate when they make a mistake. This lets them know their value outside of the mistake. When someone makes a mistake, they usually experience the feeling of disappointment followed by the anticipation of rejection. Bringing a teammate out of that place of rejection is the best thing you can do in a moment of disappointment. When selflessness is a part of the culture, there will be self-accountability. This means the team will hold themselves and each other accountable versus having the boss or the coach be the enforcer. The only way to have that awareness of others is to have a positive voice in your own head. When the people on your team want others to be more successful than themselves, everyone will win.

"3 R's of Selflessness"

Reminder. This pillar is important, because there will be highs and lows as players compete for playing time throughout the season. While there should be healthy competition within the team, there should also be a focus on team preparation to compete against others. Individually, players must stay encouraged and continue to push themselves and each other throughout the season.

Routine. The routine that must be integrated within the culture and repeated daily is the positive self-talk and encouragement within and between players. There will be daily obstacles that they must be able to push through while also pulling those beside them to be at their best. Iron sharpens iron.

Reward. Your goal is to get your team to compete every single day with a commitment to being selfless in your pursuit of success. With focused competition, the team will become better at each task as they rally for elite and consistent execution.

II. DISCIPLINE

Breakdown

Gratitude is a determining factor in the achievement of anything good. First, you have to recognize what an opportunity it is to be in the room. This allows you to operate in a state of taking full advantage of the moment. When you are disciplined, you take advantage of those opportunities to get better every day. Opportunities come every day, not just on game day. You must set and write active, measurable, and tangible goals. This creates a visual of what you hope to accomplishment. It puts the destination in the navigation. Anything that is not a step towards your goals is a misstep, and you will pay for it in the currency of time. Update and track your steps and progress. Results make it hard to fake or lie to yourself. So, set your goals, believe in them, live them out, and reward yourself for accomplishing them.

Culture Notes

1. With a negative mindset, we often do not focus on discipline and goals. We end up spending too much time in a state of fear and forget what we have.

    - The accomplishments of achieving smaller goals can help you overcome fear and put you closer to your larger goals. Build momentum throughout the Season by rewarding players for accomplishing smaller and shorter-term goals.
    - Repetition breeds discipline and discipline breeds progress.

2. You must set goals and actively pursue them. This helps you avoid distractions.

- Written goals have a higher chance of being kept and achieved.
- Set goals for the month, week, Pre-Season, and Season. Post it for all to see.
- Because the Season is long, shorter-term goals are easier to digest and maintain discipline. Always track your progress.

Story

As a young player in high school, I remember the day I sat in my room and wrote up the exact things I wanted to accomplish in the coming years of my high school basketball career. I did not play my freshman year, so I didn't think I was even on the minds of my coaches. One of my goals was to be the leading scorer on varsity, and another goal was to be the #1 player in the country. I put this list of goals over my doorway and tapped it every time I walked out the door. As a coach, I've had teams post their goals in their lockers to remind them of what they are trying to accomplish. They get to look at it every day, and it sets a guide for where to consistently channel their energy.

Summary

Put a destination in your navigation. Discipline comes from knowing what you want and directing your energy in the right place to get the results you desire. With so many daily thoughts, it's nearly impossible to be consistent without a friendly reminder or visual. Seeing your destination or goal also makes it tangible and real. It becomes harder to lie to yourself about your progress when you are looking at where you should be every day. But, knowing what you have to do is not enough; you must do it. The small things actually end up being the BIG things. No matter how small, the details add up over time. If you are doing the right things or navigating in the right direction, you will get to your destination at some point. There is no guarantee for results, but you can build the house brick-by-brick on whatever foundation you choose. Jim Rhone once said, "Things that are easy to do are also easy not to do."

"3 R's of Discipline"

Reminder. The discipline pillar is important, because disciplined goal setting gives you a destination. A Season is a marathon, and you have to chip away at the goal day-by-day. As you take steps toward your goal, you must stay the course to have a true measurement of your progress. You will do this with small daily disciplines.

Routine. The Routine to execute this pillar is to have a destination in your navigation. Writing team goals and posting in a place of high visibility. Celebrating the wins along the journey to the destination builds momentum towards the goal. It pushes you through on the tough days that lie ahead during the grueling Season.

Reward. Your goal in this pillar is to get your team to buy into the consistent activity needed to achieve success for them and for the team. They must push beyond their limits to accomplish their goals. If your team can visually see the goals, they can reach for them with a purpose.

III. TIME MANAGEMENT

Breakdown

Time, as discussed in the Pre-Season, is our most valuable asset. This is even more true during the Season. How you spend that time and prepare dictates your results. The results put you in a position to be found. Each step, no matter how small, helps propel you toward the pursuit of the ultimate goal of being successful. Acts like being on time builds trust and that goes a long way with bosses and coaches. The fact that a coach/boss knows you will be there when needed is all a part of getting an opportunity. This dependability is clutch during the Post-Season run.

Once you build the trust, you become more comfortable in the environment which opens up many options to show what you can do. Being on-time is also a function of discipline. If you can be disciplined with your time, you will be disciplined in your strategy to get success. In sports, every second, minute, and possession determines the outcome of a game. So, if you show that you value time, that value ultimately translates into success.

Culture Notes

1. Time is the most valuable asset of all.

    - The way that you manage time determines your long-term outcomes.
    - The way you manage time also helps you put yourself in a position to be ready for opportunities. Coaches often call up players

to switch combinations, and how the players have spent their time will show coaches that they are ready when they get their chance to shine.

2. Being on time build trust, reliability, and accountability.

- Coaches want players they can depend on to be floor and locker-room leaders.

3. You must often sacrifice time doing other things to invest in the team goals.

- Time is limited, so how you choose to spend your time is important.
- You must also consider the return-on-investment of your time.

Story

My first season as a women's basketball coach was a challenge. We had very little experience at the Division II level. We only had one player who had played more than ten minutes a game on the roster. And, on top of that, I was allowed to start coaching after the Pre-Season had ended. We had no idea what we were putting on the court. We had a freshman who started the year as the 16th player in the rotation, but she did everything right. More importantly, she was never late and attempted to do everything we asked.

With her short time on the court, she impacted the game on most possessions. She filled gaps we desperately needed to fill – which were defense and rebounds. She never once complained and led by example by being one of the most punctual players on the team. Meanwhile, there were transfers that played her same position that came just before practice, right before the bus left, or left early. That freshman's discipline with time translated into an opportunity, and she was able to contain the opposing team's leading scorer to lead us to the semi-finals game in the tournament.

Summary

Everything is about timing. Being ready when your number is called is important. In the coaching industry, you can go from making $15,000/year to adding a "0" in a matter of months. There is a saying that you can "be in the right place at the right time." Some coaches may say that their team started "clicking at the right time." Because we never know when that time will be, we must practice habits of managing time properly and being timely in all that we do. Being on time makes you reliable. And, being reliable is important as the long season wears on.

If I can depend on you to be there, we now have trust. Think about how disappointed you feel when someone says they will help you or do something for you and they don't – even if the reason is valid. Now, imagine them doing it over and over again. Wouldn't that cause you to not call on that person in the future situation? I'm a true believer in how you do anything is how you do everything. So, if you can't be relied upon to arrive at the right time, why would I rely on you in a high-pressure situation to make the right decision?

"3 R's of Time Management"

Reminder. This pillar is important because preparation and time go hand-in-hand. The preparation each week for a new opponent or new task is the determining factor in the outcome. Results are in the preparation.

Routine. The Routine to execute this pillar is setting an expectation of time that everyone adheres to. Some coaches say, "Being early is on time; being on time is late; and, if you're late, you may as well not even show up." You must emphasize the value of time.

Reward. Your goal is to put your team in a position to maximize their ability to perform instinctually. By instilling the time management pillar during the Season, you will prepare your players to be on the same page and perform in a more disciplined manner as you enter the Post-Season.

IV. RESPONSIBILITY & ACCOUNTABILITY

Breakdown

Everything you do involves a choice or decision. You will have many options to choose from on how to get a job or task done. When in a team setting, your decisions affect all those around you and carry consequences or rewards. Making good choices as you strive to reach your goals is a very important part of success. During the Season, things begin to move very fast as you cram practices, travel, and games into each day and week. It is important to reinforce the importance of each player holding themselves accountable and being responsible for their deposits or withdrawals into the team tank.

It is easier to be coached when you know your strengths and limitations. At this point, you can take the lead on holding yourself accountable and course-correcting in the right direction. This level of independent thinking is an asset for teams as the intensity of the games increases. This awareness helps players adjust to certain challenges. Being responsible and accountable also reminds a player of what they can control and what they cannot. This pillar can also alleviate a lot of stress and frustration.

Culture Notes

1. You have choices about how you spend your time, how you treat your body, your attitude, and how you treat others.

    - Your choices early in the Season impact your

success later in the Season.
- Being responsible and accountable does not mean you will not make mistakes, but it means that you should respond with corrective action before someone has to remind you.

2. Once you know who you are (inside); you don't have to worry about outside acceptance.

- You are more likely to accept criticisms and constructive feedback if you know your strengths and weaknesses.
- Players learn how to play for one another.

Summary

The big question here is, "What is your job?" Players and people often get caught up in an imaginary situation, because they never clearly identify what they are trying to accomplish. If everyone focuses on their job and responsibility, they can be held to an expectation of doing their job. This is critical as you reinforce the pillars of your culture during a time when everyone's contributions matter. This pillar allows you to coach more effectively and be coached when needed. Self-awareness is an important part of growth. Ultimately, you can only control what you can control, understand what you can understand, and be aware enough to change who you can change—YOU.

Story

Oftentimes, when speaking to players about mistakes, they seem to miss important details about what happened. Their response to making a mistake is to over-compensate or do nothing at all. During a game, one of my players was out of position in our defensive scheme. She came to the sideline and explained that she was in the help-side position, because her teammate was out of position. My response was, "Ok, but what was your job?" That's because if you are focused on someone else's task or job, you're taking away from your own. So, you now have multiple people doing something we didn't practice and neither knows what the other is doing. If you know how your teammates think and you know who you are you can hold them accountable. But if you are not doing your job, how can you help and/or correct them?

"3 R's of Responsibility and Accountability"

Reminder. This pillar is important because through the journey there will be choices at every turn. The decisions you make with the choices you are faced with will determine the outcome and how close you get to the goal. During the Season, wrong turns can hinder growth and success.

Routine. The Routine to execute this pillar is holding the team accountable for their decisions. When the team knows the "why," it makes it easier to make the right decisions. Encourage players to hold one another accountable to sharpen their focus. Offer rewards for players who make good decisions. This will reinforce and incentivize being responsible and accountable.

Reward. Your goal is to get your team to make the right decision as often as possible. The right decision is not only what you repetitively practice, but the ability to make the next best decision if things don't go as planned or rehearsed.

V. SMALL CIRCLE

Breakdown

During the Season, there will be many mental battles. It is always "YOU" vs "YOU." You make laws, constructs, and agreements with yourself in every aspect of your life. These principles hold YOU to your own standards to keep yourself consistent, give you direction, and hold you to the standard that YOU see fit. YOU have to answer to YOU. YOU have to look at yourself in the mirror and sleep at night according to how you uphold these standards. The inner voice in your mind is the loudest. Speaking positively to yourself in a world full of doubt and doubters will make the difference in your success.

In addition, the people around you automatically become a part of your battle team. They can help or hinder your success. Surrounding yourself with people who are positive and who support you is important to your success. It's impossible to block everything and everyone out, but the rules for who can penetrate your space and your mental fortitude to uphold those boundaries is all that you can control. By keeping a small circle, you will keep people around you who are like-minded and who will support your vision.

For coaches, the Season is a critical time to initiate conversations with your players to "check-in." In the busyness of the Season, outside voices can filter into the team dynamic and disrupt chemistry and overall well-being. As the leader, you must be intentional about asking your players about their mental health or any things they are struggling with to ensure they are leaning on healthy supports.

Distractive voices become attractive when they are challenged or mentally fatigued.

Inverse: On the other end of the spectrum are those that tell you everything you want to hear. They are just as bad as those tearing you down. They give you a false image of who you are and what you are. This can be just as, if not more, detrimental to your success.

Culture Notes

1. You are obligated to protect yourself from harm and harmful influence.

    - You should create laws for yourself that govern how you behave and who you allow around you.
    - Sometimes, the hardest word to master saying is "No!"
    - Your voice should be the loudest – not some else's.

2. When you set goals for what you want to accomplish, you should include who should be a part of that journey.

    - Surround yourself with people who have your best interests at heart.
    - Surround yourself with people who are positive, successful, and who know who you really are.

3. Beware of people who tell you what you want to

hear.

- These people give you a false image of what and who you are.
- This can be just as detrimental to your growth as having a negative voice in your circle.

Story

Players who come to college are often the best players on their high school teams, at their schools, from their hometowns, and oftentimes from their families. Having a team full of good players invites an extended family that is in full support of their success. However, when success has a bar that is set by points and playing time, it affects the player and the family. It is important that the player has the right people in their ear/circle so that the message is consistent. A circle of people or supporters that take your side in negative ways is detrimental to your success and the team's success. You must be honest about the role people play in your life.

Having a small circle isn't just about the number of people; it's the people that contribute most to your success in that playing arena. In most cases, your mother may not be a basketball expert. But, she may convince you that you need to shoot. However, you know there is much more to the game. You may have multiple small circles—your family and your team. Those two circles may collide, but it is up to you to understand the differences between them and when to tap into each one. I coached a player in high school whose parents, supporters, and AAU coaches had a different agenda than our coaching staff. They were very open about expressing this on many occasions. As a coaching staff, we truly believed that he was better than he performed at times. In practice, he was easily one of our top players. During games, he was clearly one of the bottom players. It seemed the main thing holding this player back was his ability to make quality decisions during the game.

It was clear that he had people in his circle who were distracting to him. On the one hand, he had his coaches telling him to run a play or make a certain pass for the betterment of the team. On the other hand, he had his mom and his AAU coach telling him to shoot every time the ball hit his hands. You can only imagine the negative tone during the post-game car rides or phone conversations when discussing his performance. The relationship dynamics of these circles of influence probably put the player in a difficult spot. It is hard for any player to make instinctual decisions during games with three conflicting voices in his or her head. As expected, he was never able to live up to his potential. The high school coach was blamed because he could not afford to keep him on the floor. But, the reality is his coach did not allow him to do the things that his mother and his AAU coach wanted him to do.

Summary

As the Season wears on, there will be people who want to jump on the bandwagon to your success when they see momentum. There will also be people who want to lure you off your team's ship for a variety of selfish reasons. Keeping a small circle is important to keeping you focused and committed to the culture established in the Pre-Season. Any disruption or distraction can be disastrous, and this type of disruption can spread throughout the entire team like a cancer.

Your small circle includes you and everyone around you. You must be intentional about the people who can get close to you. The voice in your head is the loudest and most convincing voice, but the people around you can also drown out your voice if you allow them. You must practice the voice in your head being positive and firm. The day-to-day practice of positivity builds confidence even when the trials and tribulations of the season begin to mount. If that first voice isn't established and clear, the other voices become the loudest. And, that is when the potential for harmful influences to take over presents itself.

"3 R's of Small Circle"

Reminder. This pillar is important because the people you surround yourself with typically have an impact on your thoughts and approach to life. There are people who are outside of the team's culture that infiltrate it by depositing thoughts into the individuals. Those thoughts manifest into decisions and reactions. You see what you want to see to feel safe in your securities and insecurities.

Routine. The Routine to execute this pillar is to have talks with your team often about not only your culture but their other cultures and circles. Know who influences them and who they talk to most frequently. This allows you to better understand and respond to contradicting views.

Reward. Your goal is to get and keep your team running as one unit. Deflect the outside and selfishness of those around them. Make the team goals louder than any other noise they may hear from people, social media, or any other source of influence.

VI. CHAMPIONSHIP EFFORT

Breakdown

Everyone has a role – big or small – in every game or practice. In the same way that a remote control will not work properly without good batteries being installed properly, everyone must be in the proper place and perform accordingly for everyone to achieve success. Every button, every screw, and every bolt is necessary for the function of the team. Each person must figure out how, within their skill set, they can help the team or group. No one would be there if the coach or leader didn't feel like they could contribute in some way.

As a leader, it is partially your job to pull the greatness out of them. But, the other part of the job is for you to bring your best to give them a fair assessment of what they're capable of. This is how all members of the team become reliable. At this point in the Season, players often face obstacles that they must dig deep to overcome. Failure is part of being a champion, it's a part of any process. You must get comfortable with both success and failure. Talk about it, face it, and grow. Champions know that hard work breeds confidence. Confidence breeds success. And, success breeds expectations and accountability. That's what champions are made of.

Culture Notes

1. Figure out how you can help your players maximize their championship effort.

- Help your players find a niche and be good at it.
- Everyone needs guidance; even the greatest players in the world had trainers.
- Remind them of their skills and how they contribute to the team.

2. Having championship effort is about being reliable.

- The players who give effort every day are the ones who will lead the team when the Season gets tough.
- As a leader, you may motivate them be expanding their role when they have proven to be reliable in a certain area. This can be used as a motivating incentive.

3. Failure and success are mutually exclusive.

- Normalize conversations around both failure and success.
- A coach-led team is good; but a player-led team is great.

4. There are some factors linked to success.

- Success is related to motivation, confidence, and routines.
- Some ways to inspire success are to use imagery to visualize success, to use motivational talk, and to model success habits.
- Arguing with officials, making excuses, and a

lack of confidence are signs that players are not giving championship effort consistently.

5. Some people fear success more than failure.

- Many players exhibit signs of anxiety as they perform when they fear success.
- There are relaxation techniques to help calm these anxieties, such as deep breathing, stretching, using music, and meditating.

Story

The mind is powerful. Have you ever noticed that when you make up your mind that you want something, your mind will become consumed with it? For example, if you've ever picked a car that you wanted, do you notice that you begin to see it everywhere? The same applies to life and success. The more you visualize your goals and positive outcomes, the more that you will begin to see the doors that open them. This visualization guides your thought processes and the level of effort that you put in every day.

In one of our championship seasons, we showed a previous team cutting the nets and celebrating the championship that should have been ours. Our goal was to have our guys visualize every detail of the moment after we completed our goal of winning. We went as far as finding all of our ring sizes and writing them down as preparation for when we won. Guess what? We went on to win the championship! We had one vision, and even though we had a slow start to the season, we ended up where we saw ourselves – as champions.

Summary

Championship effort is just as much mental as it is physical. Seeing yourself in a certain place and accomplishing something is a big part of the road to success. You have to put the "destination into your navigation." Then, your navigation system will tell you all the turns you need to make as well as the speed traps ahead. There are multiple ways to get anywhere, but I'm sure that if you want to get there in a timely and efficient manner, you don't want to have to reroute. Once you have a plan of action, you can determine which turns or steps to take to get to your goals. You can channel your energy in the direction of things that will get you closer to your goal or destination.

Each player or group member has a job on this route towards the destination. Figure out how you can help and be relied upon. If you do that consistently, your role or playing time can be expanded or more valuable. Success is not a win or a loss; it's a journey or a process. Failure is a part of that journey or process. Speak about it, embrace it, and grow from it. Make having a championship effort a habit. There is no right or wrong way to win a championship, but there is a process or formula to put yourself in a position to find success.

"3 R's of Championship Effort"

Reminder. This pillar is important, because it sets the daily bar of what it takes to be a champion. It emphasizes how important each part of this process is and what effort it takes to do it to the best of your ability. You are preparing to win the championship every single day.

Routine. The Routine to execute this pillar is to make it clear what championship effort is both mentally and physically. Set that bar and create the expectation as a coach. Players will rise to your level of expectation for them. Set the bar. Maximize effort. Repeat.

Reward. Your goal is to get your team to give a certain level of effort and for that to be the standard – the championship standard. You want them to give the same effort as they would in the championship game each day in practice.

VII. EMBRACING THE PROCESS

Breakdown

Don't let success go to your head or allow failure to go to your heart. It's an infinite game, and it tests you along the way to measure where you are. The goal throughout this process is to be ready for the test. You must be comfortable with being wrong. It allows you to grow and opens your thoughts to new ideas. I must say this again, you must embrace failure because it's part of the process. Recovery is a key element to anyone being able to perform at a high level both physically and mentally. Your work, your focus, your rest, and your consistency are just small pieces to the larger puzzle.

Most players and coaches put so much weight on the games that they do not prepare themselves or their players properly. They channel their mental energy in the wrong direction at the wrong time. There is a difference between practice time versus performance time. Practice is for repetition and getting the act executed correctly by trying different ways until you get it right. Performance is taking that correction and putting it into action with goals of perfection. Be patient with the process; your opportunities to grow come every day.

Culture Notes

1. You must remain obsessed with competition versus the result.

- This keeps you focused on the things in your

control – your daily activity.
- Don't let success go to your head or failure to go to your heart.

2. You will get it wrong sometimes.

   - Normalize both failure and success through your talk and expectations.
   - Being wrong is how you learn and grow. It is a part of the process.
   - There is risk involved in trying to accomplish something great.
   - This is why you practice.

3. While the process may look differently for everyone, it has the same components.

   - You must work hard consistently. You also need to consume the right foods and get the proper rest.

4. Embracing the process is not just for you; it's for everyone around you.

   - As you get better, you have a responsibility to help those around you get better, too.
   - What you practice and how you practice are equally important to the success of the unit.

5. There are signs of embracing the process.

   - When you embrace the process, you will see

it in your body language, your attitude, your tone of voice, and your interactions with teammates.
- When you reject the process, you will have a negative mindset, be detrimental to the team, and fail to reach your potential.
- Embracing a process is the opposite of instant gratification. It takes time.

Story

As we go through practice each day, I have watched guys work out and observed their regiments and habits. As a player, I would often hear stories about Kobe Bryant, and his goal to perfect things through repetition. As I watched our players shoot, I saw that they got bored with success. For example, they would shoot shots and make several three-pointers in a row, then shoot the next few shots differently. It was almost as if they'd made enough shots to be satisfied. The goal is to make the shot much more than you miss it. In this case, it seemed as if the players' goal was to have a good celebration after a made basket or two. Maybe their goal was to look cool. It was as if they valued that more than making the basket. When you are embracing an ongoing process, you must build consistency around the work. In the Season, this prepares you for success.

Summary

The goal is to "stack days." This means you want to line up as many good days in a row as possible. There will always be an "off-day," but we always look to minimize them. The more "good" days we can have in a row, the more consistent we can be for a longer period of time. This creates a culture of good days that count towards our success. Embracing the process means embracing the ups and downs while remaining level-headed. Being in the right mind state throughout the different phases of the Season is the key to maximizing your time and efficiency. Stacking days is important in such a way that the more "good" days you build the more it becomes a habitual ritual. From practice-time to performance-time, the gap of emulation should become smaller as the season goes on. Don't get bored with success or discouraged by failure. They are both a part of the process.

"3 R's of Embracing the Process"

Reminder. This pillar is important because success is a process. There is no instant outcome or no guarantee that things will always run smoothly. You have to embrace the ups and downs of the process in order to grow. From preparation to recovery, success, and failures, it's all a part of the overall process.

Routine. The Routine to execute this pillar is to break down the process of why you are doing what you are doing and what the results will be if you do it right and at a high level. Reiterating the why and what repeatedly helps the team remain committed to the goal.

Reward. Your goal is to get your team to make every part of the process a priority. Every part is important to the overall outcome. You may not always get it right, but you want to make consistent progress toward your goals.

POST-SEASON

Post-Season

The Post-Season is when you must execute all the pillars of the Season at a high level. Unfortunately, not all teams make it this far. The time immediately following the Season/Post-Season is one of the most important "seasons" of the year. This is when you pause to reflect on what transpired throughout the year. What worked? What didn't? This is when you listen to learn exactly where to make adjustments as you begin to prepare for your next journey to success. Sometimes, people overlook the importance of this part of the process. One important component of leadership is listening. As the leader of your program, if you aren't listening, you likely aren't learning. Because it is your job to pull the best from those under your leadership, you have to continuously look for ways to inspire them to embrace the culture.

This section of the book is written as prompts to guide your end-of-season meetings, interviews, and conversations with your players. You should conduct these individually and as a group. You want to give the players space to be honest as you continue to build trust and make them feel included in the goal-setting process. Just like your players are growing, you are expected to grow as a coach or leader.

1. How was the season? Individually and as a team?

2. Did you feel you had a fair and even opportunity to contribute?

3. What would you have considered to be a "good" season?

4. What were your goals for the season? Did you reach them? What prevented you from accomplishing your goals?

5. How did you feel about your role/contribution? What would you do differently?

6. What did you feel were your strengths?

7. What did you feel were your weaknesses?

8. What did you learn during practice that translated to the game?

9. What pregame routine did you do most consistently or did you feel worked best?

10. What post-game routine did you do on good days/bad days?

11. How did you manage and overcome off or down days?

12. What could you have done better and how?

13. What is your main improvement goal over this offseason?

Coaching Evaluation

At the conclusion of the season, coaches often make many adjustments based on the player's performance and feedback. But, many times, they fail to give their players an opportunity to assess the effectiveness of their coaching style and strategies. This section outlines a scale for players to rate their coach based on the four intelligences.

Every person learns in four primary ways: by listening (auditory), by watching (visual), by practicing (kinesthetic), and by applying skills in real-time (integration). As coaches teach and develop their players, they must be intentional about appealing to all the senses to foster deep learning. This multi-faceted teaching style helps players learn in a way that enables them to operate independently and utilize what they have learned in real time.

(For players to assess the coach)
Rate on a scale of 1-10 and explain why.

Auditory: Verbal instruction

1. How well did I give instructions?
2. Were they clear and easy to understand?
3. How can I improve my practice and game coaching style?

Visual: Film/white board/coaching demonstration

1. Did I break down the film in a way you could understand?
2. Do my gametime clipboard notes make sense?
3. How can I improve the way I teach plays and schemes?

Kinesthetic: Guided practice/independent repetition

1. Do my practice styles help you learn?

2. Do you think you or your teammates get enough reps of plays or individual work?
3. Do the practices feel like games? How can I make them better?

Integration: Role-play/simulation/real-life application

1. Do you feel that the practices prepare you for the games?
2. How can I give you more freedom to develop and create?
3. How can I help you "think" the game?

OVERTIME

Overtime

Although this book is broken down into three time periods throughout the sports year – the Pre-Season, Season, and Post-Season – the building and integration of your culture is a year-round process. Your players need to know that you care about them enough to forge relationships with them beyond the transactional nature of their performance for you. There will be times when you can create opportunities to bond with them and earn their trust. This bonding usually translates to the sport. They will trust your judgment and follow your lead more readily when they know you care.

In this Overtime section, I have shared some team activities that you can implement to connect with your players outside the game. These activities are just a few examples of team-building exercises that you can use during team functions and get-togethers. Some of the most successful teams I have been a part of or led felt like family. This is how you make the culture of your program stick.

Birthday Line

How to: Get your players to line up in order of their birthday. Players must figure out where they should line up.

Goal: To get your players to find ways to communicate with each other and be creative, while bonding.

Key Rules: The players must do this without verbal or numerical communication (motioning numbers with fingers).

Never Have I Ever

How to: Someone (preferably a coach) starts by saying "never have I ever" and finish the statement with something they've never done or experienced. The players and coaches are to stand up if they have ever done it. It can also go the opposite way. The person can say something that they HAVE done, and the people that have done it will also stand.

Goal: Have fun conversation while getting players to bond on how they are both similar and different.

Key Rules: As a coach, your job is to start the conversation with things that are funny and informative that players will be comfortable exposing. As the game goes on, you may ask more intimate, serious, or thought-provoking questions to delve deeper into the players past experiences and philosophies.

This conversational game bonds the players and coaches by their experiences while helping them learn about each other. If played properly, they will realize they have more in common and share similar experiences. It will also help them communicate with each other and build trust in a safe environment.

Goal Exchange

How to: You will give your players a specific number of questions to answer (for example, 5). The questions may vary according to the information you would like to obtain. After collecting the questions and answers, you will pass them out randomly to each player and have them read who it's from and the question and answer. Whichever teammate has the card is now responsible to hold that player accountable for working towards the goals written on the card.

Example: What are your individual goals coming into the season? What are your team goals?

Goal: The goal is to use goal-oriented questions to get a gauge of what the player is invested in coming into the season. You and the other players get to know how one another thinks and how their perspectives influence their actions.

Keys: By having the players articulate their goals and understand their teammates' goals, they can push one another to work harder and stay focused. They can also guide them to reach them. Accountability is the key.

Players are often not on the same page, because they don't take the time to understand what motivates the person beside them. If they know what each of their teammate's goals are, they will be more understanding of why they act, interact, or react the way they do in the various situations throughout the season. A player-coached team has the best chance of being successful as they hold each other accountable. This makes each individual an extension of the coaching staff.

Get to Know Them

How to: Give each player a set of questions. Try to keep it to about five for time's sake. These questions should consist of things about their family and more about their personal life outside of basketball. Collect the answers. Take one interesting question from each of them. Mix the chosen questions up and have the players guess which teammates it belongs to. You may add a prize for correct answers for motivation.

Goal: To learn more about your players. The activity also helps them learn more about each other.

Key Rules: The more the players know about each other, the stronger the bond and understanding they will have. This will give them a fun way to learn things they didn't know about each other. Most of the time we spend with our players (and they spend together) is surface level. Sometimes, we never really get to know the person and what they may have gone through.

As much as they expose themselves, there is always a deeper level that they are not willing to expose. The pressure of social acceptance and judgment will stop them from exposing more intimate details about themselves. Yet, when everybody is doing it in a safe and controlled environment, they will be more comfortable sharing around people they will be spending a lot of time with throughout the course of a season. The more bonded the players feel, the more they will play "for" each other as opposed to "with" each other.

About the Author

Coach Mo is currently the associate head coach for the women's basketball team at Young Harris College. He brings over a decade of championship experience to the program, having coached both men and women teams at the collegiate level. Coach Mo has elevated programs at Livingstone College, Christopher Newport University, and Harcum College amongst others. In his role as a scouter, recruiter, and player development coach, Coach Mo has produced several All-Americans, pushed his team to several post-season appearances, and led his programs to championships. Coach Mo is a winner.

In addition to being a champion coach, Coach Mo also has a long track record of success as a player. He spent three seasons playing basketball internationally, earning league honors each year. Prior to his professional basketball career, Coach Mo led a storied career at Longwood College. As the first-ever Division I player to leave the school, Coach Mo finished as a top-five all-time leader in scoring, rebounding, steals, assists, and blocks.

He was named Male Athlete of the Year and recognized by ESPN as one of the school's top five greatest players of all time.

Coach Mo earned his bachelor's degree in sociology from Longwood in 2013. He is recognized by many as a rising star in collegiate basketball. In addition to his sports success, Coach Mo hosts a podcast, sells merchandise under his I AM > brand, and inspires athletes and colleagues around the country. The championship coach hails from Virginia.

Made in the USA
Columbia, SC
06 April 2024